THE WORLD ACCORDING TO CARP

by Richard Guindon

A GUINDON COLLECTION

Andrews and McMeel, Inc.
A Universal Press Syndicate Company
Kansas City • New York

P9-EDJ-118

The World According to Carp copyright © 1983 by the Los Angeles Times Syndicate. All rights reserved. Printed in the United States of America. No part of this book may be used or reproduced in any manner whatsoever without written permission except in the case of reprints in the context of reviews. For information write Andrews and McMeel, Inc., a Universal Press Syndicate Company, 4400 Johnson Drive, Fairway, Kansas 66205.

ISBN: 0-8362-1214-2
Library of Congress Catalog Card Number: 83-71759

First printing, September 1983
Second printing, November 1983

August, 1892: J.A. Poppe, traveling from Holstein, Germany, arrives on our shores with five carp, the first to be introduced to America.

"Let's go home and watch it on T.V."

Orton Fenster, observing his register for the draft and wondering what all
the fuss is about.

So much of America has become self-service that it has just occurred to
Myron Fenster that he hasn't actually talked to anyone in four months.

"Today, I tried life in the fast lane. But all I got was a lot of cars stacked up behind me."

"In my fantasy, Pat Summerall comes home after work at the hardware store and says, 'Hi, Honey! Anything around the house need fixing?'"

"I sent you a card. I take it mine is in the mail?"

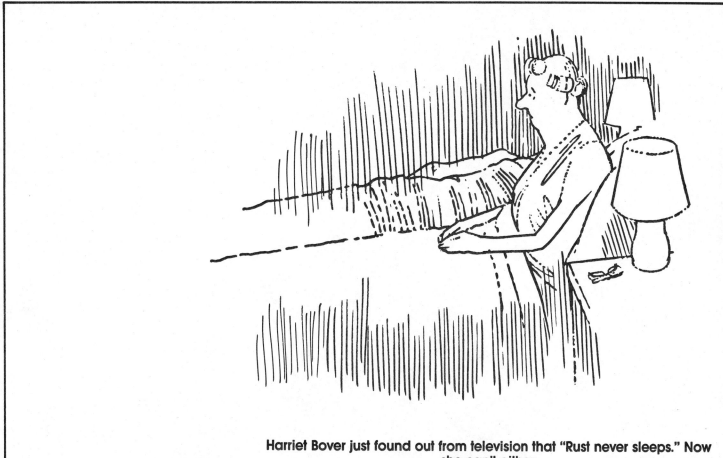

Harriet Bover just found out from television that "Rust never sleeps." Now she can't either.

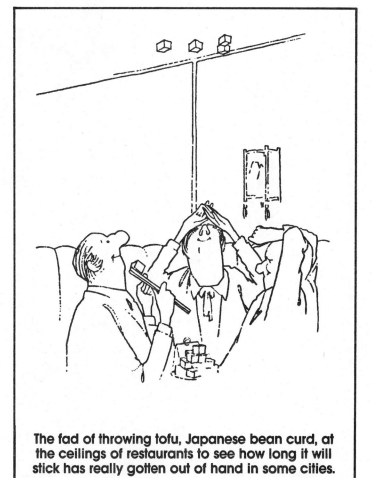

The fad of throwing tofu, Japanese bean curd, at the ceilings of restaurants to see how long it will stick has really gotten out of hand in some cities.

One capful every 4 hours.

A common restaurant scene: women taking food from men.

Henry Schultz is worried. He's found a slip of paper in his pocket which says he has been passed by inspector number 7. He figures they did it while he was asleep.

"You look better already, dear."

"We said, no pets, Mrs. Fenster."

"Richard, you're thirty now and it's time to let go of your invisible friend."

"This is me at my peak?"

Rodger Fenster is the first person to appear on the TV show "People's Court" to be sentenced to death.

Eunice Bensen defeats the Russian, Alexi Kropotkin at "Mr. Potato Head," with a brilliant 112 variations.

One of those photos that will embarrass Bea and Randy Newman ten years from now.

"Thank you, dear. That's better."

1923, the neatest thing! The invention of sliced bread!

"Why don't you let me fix you up with Harry? He can catch a frisbee in his mouth."

"If they really want us to drive 55, why not just set the speed limit at 40?"

It's exhausting to think about it, but there are millions of people, and each of us has a plan every day.

"I wish you wouldn't do that first thing in the morning."

"Mom? Dad? It's Charlie, Heather and the baby. Open up. We gotta drop the U-haul off before five."

"Hi! I'm Bob and I need someone to talk to because I've just finished this week's People magazine and my mind is racing."

Even the cynics will have to agree that one improvement made by the present administration is the Ron and Nancy look, seen here on Orton and Flo Hackett of Gainesville, Florida.

AVOCADO, GINSENG YOGURT

twinkies
twinkies
twinkies

The revolving door on the first try.

Bobby Fenster, a bounty hunter for supermarket shopping carts in Providence, Rhode Island, seen here with his longest recovery: a cart found in Scottsdale, Arizona.

One reason why you can't find a pen or pencil next to the phone when you need one.

Scientists have just discovered that in winter, carp migrate to this rather sleazy hotel in Newark, N.J.

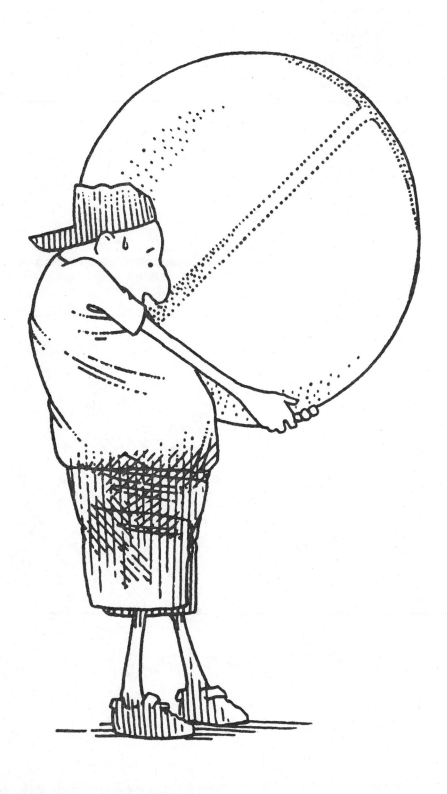

At last! An exercise pill that really works!

"Harvey, sometimes I think you're too cautious about life."

Eunice Benson, who won first prize at the state fair for her pickled beets, avoiding the press.

Another one of those disagreements over who has contributed more to
American comedy, Cheech and Chong or the Three Stooges.

Dressing for a loan: It helps if you wear something pathetically out
of season.

"Just remember to keep your head out of the water. The carp will do the rest."

"For busy families like mine who always eat and run, I spray all my food with Pam. It goes down faster."

"I wonder if sailfish have a religion that says when they die they end up on the wall of a restaurant."

"The way the economy works, if a man has ten carp and he gives four to the government, no matter how you slice it, he's still stuck with six carp."

"The nays have it. The motion to change the name of Truth Or Consequences, New Mexico, to The MacNeil-Lehrer Report is not carried."

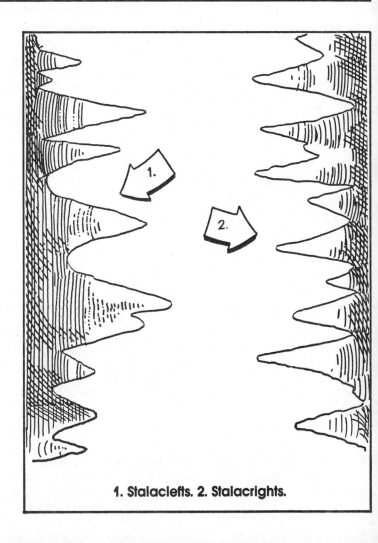

1. Stalaclefts. 2. Stalacrights.

CAMOUFLAGE
1. COUNTRY

2. CITY

"Folks, here are the keys to your new car, along with my condolences."

"Remember our first date? You got sick all over the linoleum in the car."

A typical fight in the wild over possession of a sleeping bag.

Another one of Rodney Cooney's inventions that may prove impractical—talking cocktail napkins.

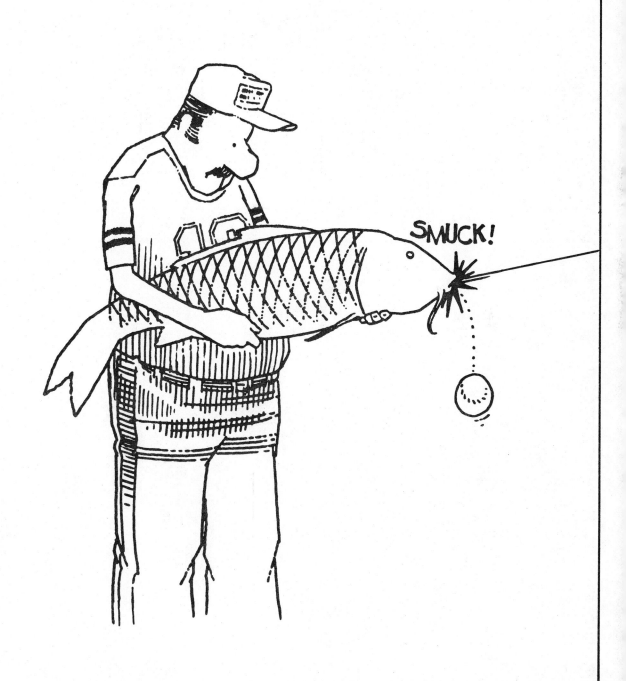

The correct way to bunt with a carp is head first.

"Mom, he was in the street, yelling, 'Hey! Show us your underalls!'"

"This is my husband, Jesse. In my fantasy he's Harry Reasoner."

Roger Blunt has been saving newspapers most of his life. Later on, he figures to make some trees.

Eunice Benson, about to go to plan "B."

The anchorman look. Let's nip this in the bud before it spreads to the general population.

Maude Brewster, one of the growing number of shoppers who wear disguises to avoid coupon embarrassment.

While carp may not be endangered, the demand for skins to make shoes and briefcases is reaching disturbing proportions.

"Very smart, those monograms. That way you don't put on your wife's clothes by mistake."

"Out": Anything in Muffie Goldstein's wardrobe.

Another one of Herman Fenster's ideas being met with ridicule
and derision.

"Goodbye. I'm leaving you, Beatrice."

Never point if you want something from another person's plate.

In learning to drive a stick shift, it's important that you first relax.

"If you have to ask, you can't afford it."

There are a few people, Milford Briggs, for example, who are so dispassionate that they have to jump up and down before they can make those heat-sensitive elevator buttons work.

MARGE PFIEFFER

"RED" NELSON

SISSY LONDON

"MIKE" FENSTER

Four people, known by the authorities, who would kill for chocolate.

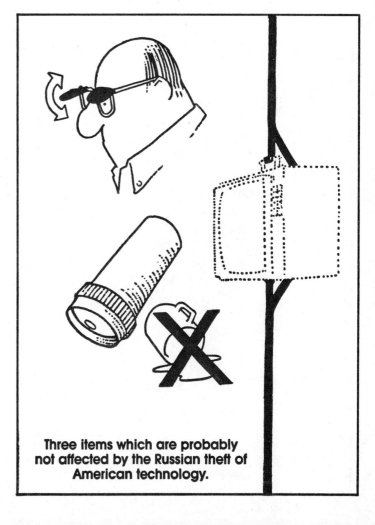

Three items which are probably not affected by the Russian theft of American technology.

Can you spot the bald man in this picture?

As far as scientists can determine, carp are the only living creatures that, apparently, have no place in the food chain.

"I wanted to get you a dog but they're too hard to wrap."

Air bags for joggers.

Some people who are not into designer clothes, make a statement about themselves by carrying their awards around with them.

"Sure, mister. Go someplace where they don't have extradition."

The news that the preppy look is fading out is being taken pretty hard in some circles.

Why look like this... when you can look like this?

George Foster, still wearing hand-me-down clothes.

"Now, if this were a formal dinner, the dog would more correctly be on a trivet."

"I can't talk now. He's here and he's with his wife."

Mrs. Eunice Benson, in a supermarket with a full shopping cart noticed the 10-items-or-less register and decided to give it a shot.

"It's beautiful. This would be a good place to bury a dog if you had to."

"This is my friend, Harry. He's into the relationship much deeper than me."

A LEGAL HOLIDAY.

AN ILLEGAL HOLIDAY.

Beets! They're not just for breakfast anymore.

Harvey Fenster shooting a documentary of Harvey Fenster.

Walter Cronkite talking back to the TV news.

"If you hadn't let yourself go, you could still be doing modeling for Hummel figures."

One reason not to start an argument with someone using Krazy Glue.

Another quiet day at the speakers bureau for the Okra Growers Association.

"I'm very, very serious when I tell you that this is the most fun I ever had on a date."

"You're not so old. I got stuff in my fridge that's older than you."

Places you can go to meet girls if you're fed up with singles bars.

Milard Ferguson figures he's got just about enough of those energy saving tips enclosed with his utility bills as he needs.

A MOVIE.

Places you might as well go to in case of imminent nuclear attack.

A native born American, a naturalized citizen and an illegal alien.

"When the car broke down, we had to walk along the highway in the dark. It's a good thing Harry was wearing his Hartz 3-in-1 tick collar which reflects oncoming car headlights."

Dealing with the cost overruns of the new Swiss army knife.

The development of the solar-powered wrist watch was not an overnight success.

"And this was Uncle Harry, who went broke trying to raise chickens for their pelts."

"My share of the bill is $4.18, you owe $6.26, and Bob, yours is $94.66."

"That's how the Japanese get all our secrets. Every one of those copiers is sending duplicates to Tokyo."

"I should warn you. I once got a refund from a carnival on some three-day-old candy floss."

Hard bargaining going on during the swap meet for leftovers.

"Hi, I'm from the private sector. You folks need any money?"

"Is it OK to drink white wine in brown shoes?"

Mildred Filmore about to begin a relationship with yet another guy on the rebound.

"I want to return this scooper. My dog refuses to use it."

The precedent set by the Supreme Court in Fenster vs Fenster established that if Mr. Fenster makes one more smart remark about Mrs. Fenster's "Tuna Ole" she gets to smack him.

You have to give Rodney Bernard credit. Despite the curves that life keeps throwing him, he always manages to land on his feet.

"Mom? Did you clean up my room, again?"

"A description of the hero in my novel. He was a tall, lean man, with a rugged handsomeness that women found irresistible. Also, he was double jointed."

"I hate the idea that everything in my drains gets all mixed in with other people's stuff."

It is socially acceptable to wear hair curlers in public if it's a Saturday. It tells the neighborhood you have a date that night.

If we are going to have judges at fashion shows, let's put some teeth into the law.

"There's no point in buying artichokes. Herman won't eat any vegetables that can't be mashed."

"It's a piece of pineapple, a slice of orange and some grapes. They do that in California where people still know how to take chances."

On the plus side, inflatable clothing will compensate for gains and losses in weight without a change in wardrobe.

The Frisbee mulcher making its rounds.

"We did pretty good with the tourists this summer ever since we changed the town's name to 'GAS, FOOD AND LODGING.'"

"You're having a paper drive?"

"You think you've had chili? Wait until you've tried the chili Eunice makes."

"Wide ties, narrow ties, white shoes, dark shoes, I got fed up."

"Do you suppose any of our stuff was ever new?"

Fish boards being cut up into fish sticks.

"Look! It's the trickle down theory and it's working!"

Never have a carp fetch a banana. They just go find it and eat it.

E.F. Hutton, trying to get a word in at home.

"Mom? How do you plug this in?"

Just because you do aerobics doesn't mean you have to suffer the music.

Have you ever noticed that albums titled, "The Best of . . ." never are?
That's because Harry Foster here makes all the selections.

"I don't mind being forgetful. The thing I hate is remembering that I forgot something."

"Plus, and I'm quite serious about this, it comes with a 73-year guarantee."

"He refuses to go to obedience school. What now?"

"It's six o'clock. No killer bees."

"We figured the invitation included the dog."

"I'm afraid your Toyota has . . . lost face."

"Happy practice. If you don't practice, you can't get happy."

"It was quite a party. I spent most of it trying to talk the radiator into playing 'Lady of Spain.'"

"Always remember to keep your sense of humor, Etta. It's the one thing that separates us from the scum."

In removing food that has passed the expiration date on the label, the proper equipment is a must.

"Excuse me. Are you my waitress?"

Three statements I never listen to.

"Quick! Kiss me. My boyfriend's coming and I'm trying to make him jealous."

"Who says that conservatives can't loosen up and have a good time when they get together?"

"Kids? I'd like to say a few words about record sales and the dangers of video games."

"It's New Year's Eve and the biggest thing that is going to happen to me is some of my coupons are going to become void."

Some employees of Consumer Reports, trying to decide the best place to have lunch.

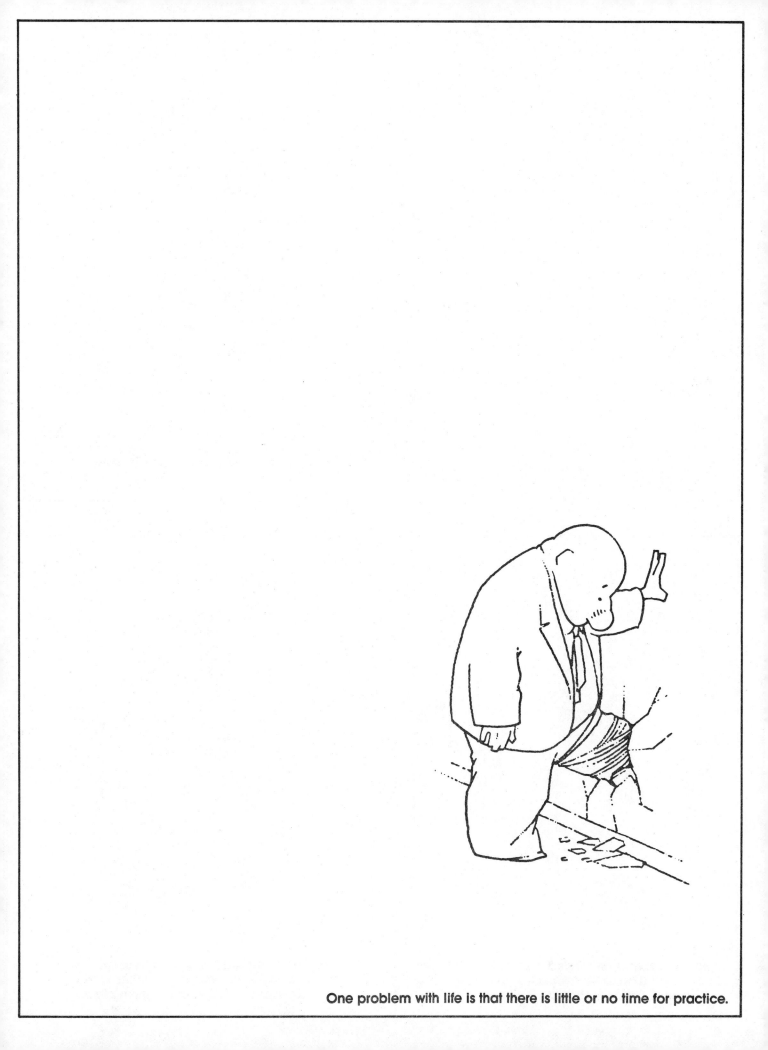

One problem with life is that there is little or no time for practice.

The carp diet. You place a carp in your refrigerator and it takes away your appetite.

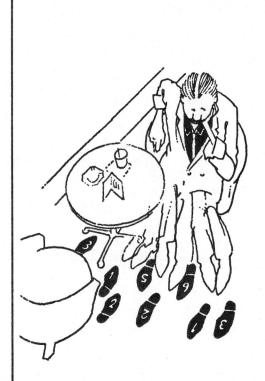

You know those people that go to discos and can't dance, but make great moves while seated? I got a friend who calls them "chair dancers."

"Hi! I'm Bert and I've dialed your number into my call forwarding service. Can we go over to your place? I'm expecting an important call."

Please disregard last week's household hint about using those two-sided, adhesive sponge squares to hold your rollers in place.

WHAT EVER HAPPENED TO... THE DOUBLEMINT TWINS ?

Divorced, they are living in a trailer park in Sarasota, Florida.

The monthly meeting of Parents Without Penguins.

You can make as many carp prints as you want because carp are not copyrighted.

Unemployed Americans sneaking into Mexico to find work.

"Oh, I get a lot of that. Most people have a preconceived idea about how a dentist should look."

"Dear, I think it's our insurance man, for you."

Johnny Carson's biggest fan must be Sadie Hollinger. She doesn't just watch the show, she buys the suits.

"Don't play with your food, dear."

"Now we owe the Fensters a carp."

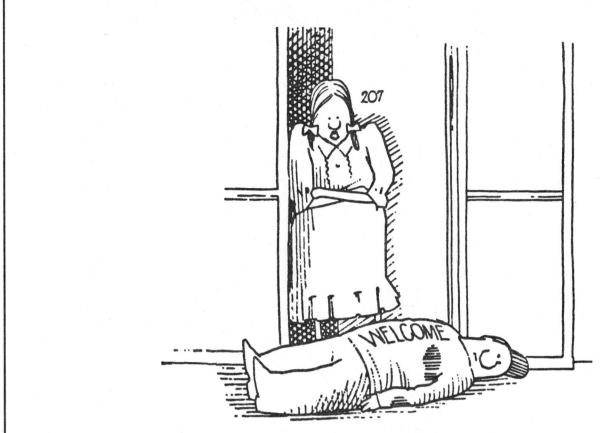

"Another reason why I won't go out with you, Harvey, is that you have such a low opinion of yourself."

Hiram Fenster, who has no bad habits, deciding to give up plaid for New Year's.

"Her telephone knows all of her secrets."

"Those were my dad's last words to me before he passed. 'Shirley,' he said, 'never whistle with your mouth full of food.'"

"One teaspoon minced onion, one teaspoon mayonnaise, and one tablespoon chopped egg. It's a recipe for egg salad that you make directly in your mouth."

Just so long as Bernie Mead takes his nap with a lot of change in his pocket, Flo Mead will always be able to find him.

Chuck Norris, tired of being stereotyped, does Hamlet.

"You can carry it off because you're big boned."

"You've seen those cute little Keebler elves who make cookies? Well, I can broccoli!"

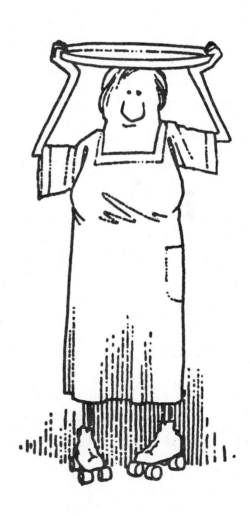

Lazy Susan. Artist conception.

"Hey, gang, it's me, Benny Burton! Remember Benny Burton? I was the shy one. You probably never noticed that I ran the projector. Guess how many times I saw 'America's Breadbasket.' I bet you can't guess . . ."

Prep for marriage. Learning the signal for shut up.

"First I was worried because I didn't know who Rula Lenska was. Now I'm worried about what happened to her."

"Hey, you got good taste! Can I have your stuff?"

"Harry, thank God you're home! 'Real People' has been trying to reach you all day."

"They're for picking up carp."

A liberal throwing money at a problem.

"Hang on to my phone number. It's unlisted. I don't want any weirdos calling me."

One more reason to be glad you didn't go into the anchovy business.

Unfortunately, okra parties don't seem to have helped the okra industry much.

"I'm terrified of being underdressed at a party. Henry feels just the opposite."

"I figure this is a savings of $7,000.00 over a store-bought hot tub."

"What would you like to hear next?"

"Just when I get backcombing down pat, they spring something new on us."

Sadie Foster, after a lifetime as a housewife and mother has decided to start living outside the law.

In barter, at the current rate of exchange, 17 carp are worth one brown vinyl wallet.

1936. Ernest Hemingway catches a carp while trout fishing and decides not to write about it.

"Let's face it, Henry, I've grown and you haven't."

"You shouldn't wallow in self-pity. But it's OK to put your feet in it and swish them around a little."

"I hate waiting. I wish time could be put in a microwave oven."

ANOTHER THING OUR AUTO EXECUTIVES DO BETTER THAN THE JAPANESE.

USE A KNIFE AND FORK.

"I like to think of myself as living proof that people have a sense of humor about themselves."

Carp fighting. When are the authorities going to crack down on this boring "sport"?

"It don't get any better than this."

Caroling the carp. A Christmas tradition in the Fenster household.

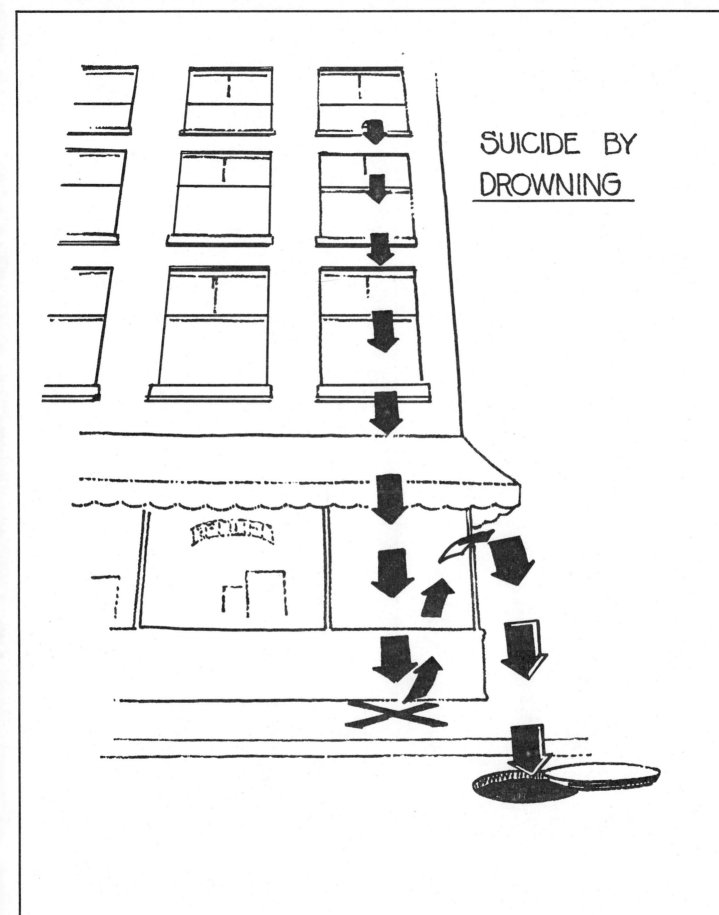

SUICIDE BY
DROWNING

VIDEO FRIEND INC.

"Him! I want to meet him!"

"Congratulations! You weren't here for the raffle, but you won me in the drawing."

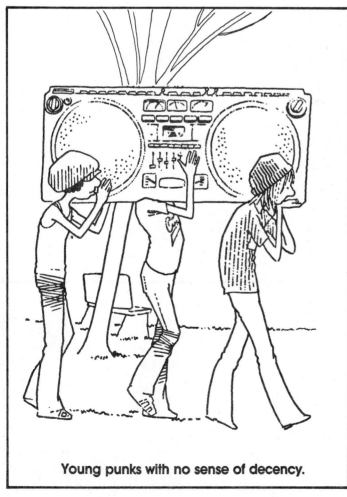

Young punks with no sense of decency.

"That was the damnedest Tupperware party I've ever been to."

"OK, go. But hurry up! That's the problem of traveling with a carp."

Betty Fenster has decided to become famous for her hair.

Polyesters usually mate for life unless the male goes to a convention. Then it's "Look out Cincinnati! Hide the women!"

"Oh, no! It looks like more trouble for Little House on the Prairie!"

"We liked the movie but Roger Ebert and Gene Siskel sitting behind us talked all the way through it."

The senior class at the Space Academy trying to remember where the graduation ceremonies are being held.

"I don't want to be a cowboy when I grow up because I detest the idea of living in a house trailer."

Things you can do that are free. Go to a department store and lie on the carpet books.

"Fenton, isn't it? Class of 81? What happened out there?"

"It's Harlequin books. They want to know how the romance novel is coming."

"There was a time when 'Made in America' meant something."

Left, Harvey Schwartz. Right, Harvey Schwartz's stunt man.

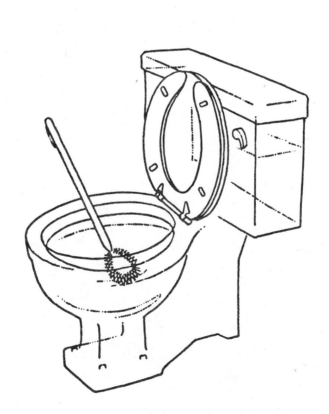

One item I'd just as soon not see made out of Lucite even in a TV commercial.

Carp are the perfect fish to wrap newspapers in.

One reason polyesters are so easily captured is that they have lousy protective coloring.

Have you noticed more and more joggers wearing bug deflectors this year?

"We got stopped at the Swiss border because Harry couldn't meet the dress code, but the rest of the trip was wonderful."

You can make your hair look like an expensive vinyl wig by using varnish.

If you are keeping a pet carp, remember to have it dry-cleaned at least twice a year.

"It is comforting to know that in Russia, you'd have to manage a rubber hat factory to qualify for a house like ours."

Yet another use for okra that seems to have been overlooked.

Sadie Hollinger keeps people from crowding her by using the grocery separator sticks found in supermarkets.

"I would like to see Aldo Cella in a wet jump suit."

"I'll pick you up at eight. Be sure to bring a book, because I'm boring."

Just as soon as Harry Bump can find a use for those Styrofoam packing forms, I think we're all going to rest a little easier.

"In our next incarnation, let's come back just as we are."

"No, I didn't take a number. I carry my number around inside me and it's next."

Going south. The carp migration.

"You're not very good at this. Did you turn state's evidence somewhere in return for a new identity as a fry cook?"

"Can I put my credit card payment on my credit card?"

His first pair of leather shoes.

"Now, remember your card and slip it back into the deck so he doesn't see it."

"I got the padded toilet seat on. Should we invite someone over?"

TOFU PRODUCTION

AMERICAN WORKER

JAPANESE WORKER

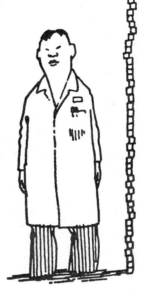

Couples who talk like a co-anchor news team.

Consumer news for the affluent.

One problem with the barter method is getting the carp in the cash register.

Hopefully, the fad going around that has people dressing "North Dakota," will soon pass.

With the help of hypnosis, Claire Fuller was able to gain fifteen pounds in the last three weeks.

Harvesters working the Silicon Valley in California.

"Knock it off! I'm trying to read."

Now, before we prepare our carp, it's a good idea to see if your tetanus shot is current."

Volunteerism: our hidden resource.

"It's 6 a.m. That's too early to pick up chicks—let's go ice fishing."

Too few people seem to be taking advantage of the Carp Stamp program.

"He was gorgeous. White shoes, matching belt, plaid on plaid. Full Cleveland!"

"Where are all the good-looking broads?"

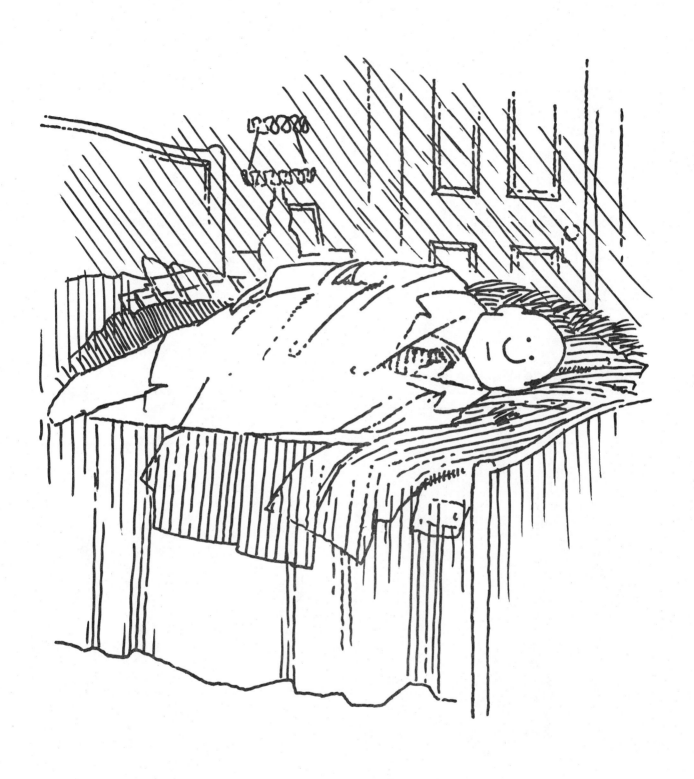

For the third time this month, Walter Norman arriving at a party has been told to throw his coat on the bed. Walter Norman is beginning to dread parties.

"That's my Henry. People either love him or hate him, there's no in-between."

The wing tip collection at Harvard.

In the Andes, high up in the mountains, Juan Valdez, spending another sleepless night because of the coffee.

"I'm completely nude, too. Who is this?"

"These are my fat clothes."

"I had to stay in last night and watch a book."

What Jimmy Connors might look like if he were a parking lot attendant.

In spring, when carp return to their birthplace to spawn, they often find no one wants to rent to them.

Martial artist.

"Since it is my first novel, I set it in one room."

While sun tea seems to work, it's probably a good idea to stay away from the sun squash.

"The pursuit of happiness is written right into the Constitution. We're supposed to be doing this."

Jane Fonda, actress, nutritionist, distributing salads to the poor.

"Thanks, we're just looking."

Carp pyramid schemes are fun, but remember to enter late. That way,
you'll get stuck with fewer carp.

Disguises that will burglar-proof your home.

"Clean up, paint up, fix up. Let's tie dye the dog."

What is more cloying than couples who wear matching outfits?

More fashion victims. How long before Nancy Reagan speaks out?

"Are you not speaking to me, dear?"

"Is this it, Flo? Is this all there is?"

SERVING NUMBER 97

Another thing robots can do better than people.

Fish kicking.

GUINDON, who doesn't understand this cartoon.

"Bea, this is Herman Foster, the inventor of the tube sock."

Kids, this is an example of what can happen when you are allowed to design yourselves as teenagers.

"Hey, Boots, jazz is back."

"Do you think our furniture is a little trendy?"

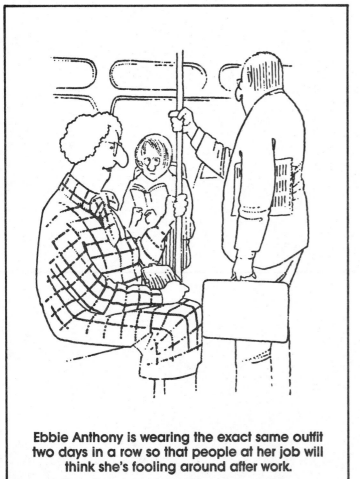

Ebbie Anthony is wearing the exact same outfit two days in a row so that people at her job will think she's fooling around after work.

What Jackie Kennedy Onassis might look like if she were a heavy-set hostess in a pancake house.

"The roads are awful. I think I hit a Smurf."

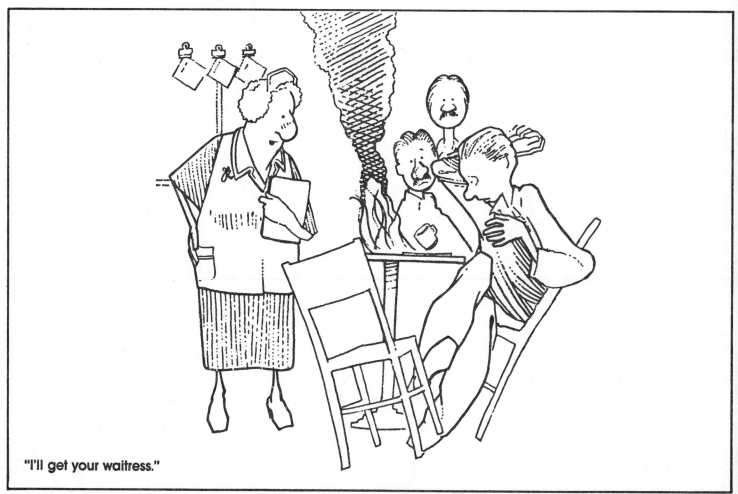

"I'll get your waitress."

Very little escapes Sadie Hollinger's attention since she began wearing her 3-D glasses.

Insulating with Jello.

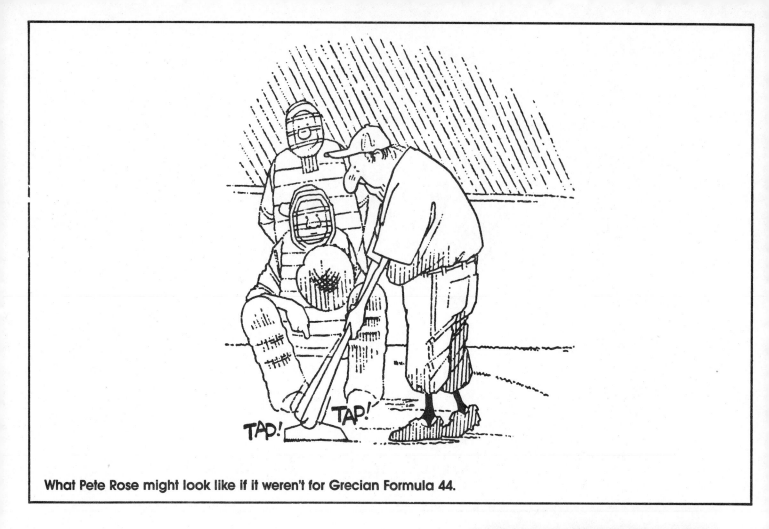

What Pete Rose might look like if it weren't for Grecian Formula 44.

The telephone company now has a hand puppet for people who hate talking on the phone.

Proof, that at sometime during their evolution, dogs passed through a stage of folk singing.

They are now using kid guides to help adults overcome computer anxiety.

"Neither of them is very handy. They're the kind of people who have aluminum foil on the rabbit ears of their TV."

Truly fast food.

IN
TUNA NOODLE
CASSEROLE.

OUT
GOING LIKE
THIS.

More in and out information.

"The newspapers keep quoting things that John Hinckley says from prison. Shouldn't they add, 'But of course we all know he's crazy'?"

"Don't think of it as a $6,000 car. Think of it as $20,000 in parts if purchased separately."

"Did anybody ever tell you that you look a little like Ralph Nader?"

Proof that dogs at some time during their evolution walked upright

A period of amnesty has been declared to allow those households with ballpoint pens from companies they never heard of, to return them.

SHE WANTED TO TALK. OK? SO I WENT OVER THERE. OK? SHE TOLD ME SHE WANTED TO BREAK IT OFF. OK?

I WANTED TO KNOW WHY. OK? SHE SAID SHE FELT I NEEDED TOO MUCH REASSUR-ANCE EVERY TIME I MADE A STATE--MENT. OK? SO I SAID...

"Henry? Guess what they want for a new Chevy 4-door?"

"Dear, I think you should stop nagging your father about the length of his hair."

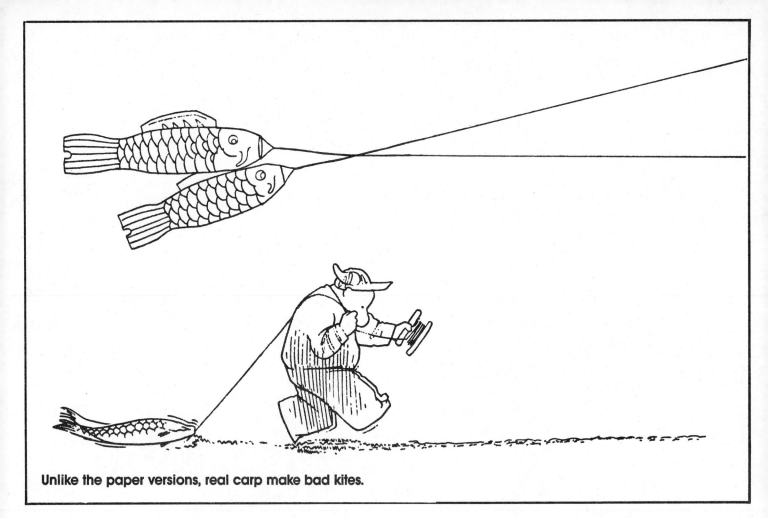

Unlike the paper versions, real carp make bad kites.

"The best way to check your house for drafts is to walk around wet-nude
with a clip board, taking notes."

"Harry doesn't have any erogenous zones and he doesn't think anyone else should."

"We're just back from vacation. The cat's not speaking to us, but the dog seems happy that we're back."

"Oh, nothing much. I was just sitting here, thinking metric."

"Sometime during the night, my face joined another generation."

"Of course, yours is not a true stocking cap."

It looks like things got out of hand again at the Annual Carp Festival in Toledo, Ohio.

"If you ever sell this business, don't you dare try to charge anything for goodwill."

Erik Estrada, as Ponch, goes undercover to break up a ring of thieves who steal condiments from restaurants.

CARRYING YOUR CARP...

right   right   wrong